DANCING ON THE EDGE
Clearly I have issues

CAROL JACOBSON

Wild Grace Publications

Published and distributed in the United States by:
Wild Grace Publishing
PO Box 270098
Louisville, CO 80027
wildgracepublishing.com

Project Editor and Interior Design: Amy Collette
Cover Design: Lee Ater
Illustration: Jodi Luce
Author Photo: Pam Taylor

Jacobson, Carol
Dancing At the Edge
ISBN: 978-0-9961692-2-6

ACKNOWLEDGEMENTS

Thank you family and friends for your love and support during this journey. Thank you to the professionals who were part of the journey. I believe we have all grown through this process and I am proud to call you friends. Thank you, dear reader, if just one poem touches you, I will consider this a success.

~ Carol

DEDICATION

How does a middle-aged hair dresser become a poet
and publish a book? She chooses to be unreasonable,
and leaves behind all of the "reasons" why she can't.
This book is dedicated to you – may you be
outrageous and unreasonable and find your dream.

~ Carol

TABLE OF CONTENTS

THE DRAGON RIDER 1

LOVE WHISPERS 3

LET SOMETHING ELSE DEFINE ME 4

HER FINAL STAND 5

FOREVER IS TOO SMALL..............................7

IT WAS IN YOU ALL ALONG 8

MY GARMENT OF SHAME 9

THE BEGINNING.. 10

THE BATTLE...................................... 11

LOOKING FOR THE BEGINNING 12

DANCE WITH ME..13

SCARED... BUT I AM NOT AFRAID 14

MONSTER OF MY HEART 15

THIS IS YOUR WARNING...........................16

THE MERMAID AND THE BOY 18

UNSHED TEARS...20

INVISIBLE PRISON 21

SILENT SCREAMS..22

THE MEASURE OF A MAN 23

MY MUSICIAN 24

LET THE THUNDER ROLL 25

YOUR MISTRESS 26

PLOT TWIST 27

LOVE'S QUESTIONS 28

LEAVE THE WORLD BETTER 29

MY DANCE WITH A DEMON 30

LIFE CAN BE LIKE THAT 31

DISTANCE BETWEEN US 32

A LITTLE TOO REAL 33

A BEAUTIFUL NIGHTMARE 34

MY LOVER THE MOON 35

LIVE OUT LOUD 36

THE QUIET IS SO LOUD 37

LOVE IS RIGHT 38

DARK KNIGHT 39

EVERY FEELING 40

I LONG FOR CONNECTION 41

THE TIME BETWEEN 42

BASKET OF LIES 43

THE DEMON ME 45

I BLAME THE MOON 46

MY SILENCE SPEAKS 47

LOVE ME FIERCELY 48

TIME TO PLAY, TIME TO PRAY 49

PRISON STEW 50

A SCARY BEAUTIFUL DANCE 51

REAL, BUT NOT TRUE 52

CLOAKED IN DARKNESS, ON MY OWN 53

RAIN BROUGHT THOUGHTS OF YOU 54

MY JOURNEY 55

DANCING ON THE EDGE 56

RAGE IS BORN 57

BEAUTIFUL 58

DON'T ANSWER HIS CALL 59

LITTLE GIRL 60

HUBRIS 61

GIRL WITH THE FATHOMLESS EYES ... 62

LET ME... 64

WHO IS WILLING? 65

KISS ME 66

JUDGE AND JURY 67

MONSTERS I KEEP 68

STORM CHASER 69

DARK DELIGHT 70

A LIFE SUSPENDED 71

IN THE END...72

OUR DEMONS DANCE 73

I AM BRAVE 74

MY SECRET PLACE..75

A STORY NEVER TOLD 76

THE QUESTION..77

AWAY 78

ONE MORE TIME...79

REBEL 80

PUPPET MASTERS 82

WILD CREATURE 83

THE BARD...84

ANYONE CAN BE A HERO...........................85

THE GIFT I RECEIVED 86

MY NORMAL NOW..87

AN INVISIBLE WALL 88

THE ILLUSIONS WE BELIEVE.....................89

DIGNITY IS BORN 90

PLAIN AND SIMPLE......................................92

THIS MASK..93

LOVE CAN CUT DEEP 94

A SMALL GIRL.................................... 95

SWEET ECHO..................................96

MONSTERS UNDER MY BED 97

NIGHT WINDS LULLABY............................98

THE STORY YOU TELL...............................99

THE STORY SOLD...100

MY HEART 101

PERHAPS 102

ALL HALLOWS' EVE 103

THAT MOMENT..104

I AM... 105

ALICE 106

OUR FEAST.. 107

BROKEN PIECES 108

MORE ME 109

MISTRESS OF THE SHADOWS.................110

I STILL FEEL...111

LIKE ME 112

A LOVE THAT COULDN'T LAST 113

RETRIBUTION 114

ALL OF YOU.. 115

A DIFFERENT TRUTH 116

A LITTLE BRAVE 117

DARKNESS, MY LOVE 118

THIS IS WHO I HAVE BECOME 119

WHO ARE YOU? 120

WILD AND FREE 121

IF ME, THEN YOU 122

THE SECRET OF THE STARS 123

THE PLACE IN YOUR HEART 124

EVEN THOUGH YOU CAN'T SEE 125

GOODBYE 126

COUNT THE COST 127

HARD LESSONS.. 128

I WISH I KNEW 129

DISAPPOINTMENT....................................130

LOVE THE SAME WAY 131

JUST TO BE...132

MY HEART AND HEAD.............................. 133

WALKING THE GLOOM............................. 134

SONG OF SILENCE 135

THANK YOU FOR NOTICING....................136

PERCY 137

A MAN WORTH KNOWING 138

ABOUT THE AUTHOR..................................139

THE DRAGON RIDER

Dragons are here to stay
You can hate them, or fight them,
      but they aren't going away
Dragon killers strap on their armor
      and head out for a fight
They have shields, swords and plans, their will, their
      strength, their might
Dragon killers believe that this is what they must do,
      try to keep their world dragon free
This might work for some, but it doesn't
      work for me...
I know if I kill this dragon another will come and take
      his place
So the time has come, to look my wretched demon in
      the face
I meet his gaze, we start to circle, the wary steps of an
      age-old dance
Each looking for strengths and weakness, each
      watching the other's stance
Patience, consistency, and respect pave the way
Conquering myself and my fears
      let me win this day
I'm a dragon rider, my demon is here to stay
But instead of being my adversary... bringing me to
      the depths of degradation

He helps me climb the tallest mountains, and lose my
      breath in exhilaration
Riding dragons, embracing your demon,
      using it to climb to new heights,
Giving up my armor, and my will,
      giving up the futile fight
That's the bravest thing I've ever done
And that's the greatest battle that I have won

LOVE WHISPERS

Whisper that you love me,
Write it on my heart
Show me that you care for me even when we're apart
Let me know you think of me in the wee hours of the
      morning
Shower me with a thousand kisses without
       any warning
Hold me tight and help me feel the feelings
       I locked away
Indulge me in some giggles and a little play
Then the next whisper of love I hear from you,
In that moment I'll believe it's true

LET SOMETHING ELSE DEFINE ME

Please don't let me be defined by my worst day
I would give anything and everything
          to take that away
Know that every war is both won and lost
Each and every battle fought comes with a cost
When I look in the mirror I can see
The eyes of condemnation looking back at me
All my sins, pride and shame
Stuck to me like they're my name
The would have, could have,
          should haves echo in my head
Tormenting me till I wish I was dead
And the why's... they keep me up at night
Why did I do it? Why didn't I choose right?
I'm sick to death of all of this
In moments I long for death's final kiss
How do I move beyond the pain,
          and the shame, and the sin?
Let something else define me,
          let something else win

HER FINAL STAND

She had smoke in her eyes and
    death was at her back
She stood alone, against all odds,
    against her the deck was stacked
She was wrapped in darkness like a cloak,
Not a whisper or a word she spoke
This day the monsters had attacked and won
She had fought hard and now she was done
The monster narrowed his eyes and
    smiled his evil grin
Death stood with his arms opened wide, welcoming
    her in
He said "Just give up, it's easy, you can't
    possibly win"
She thought of what had brought her to this place,
The ugly, the bad, the manipulation and disgrace
Giving up when you're tired and resting in death's
    embrace
Not having to fight... a type of peace she could almost
    taste
It wasn't in her to go down without a fight
If she went down, it would be swinging with all her
    might
So she squared her shoulders and looked them both
    in the eye
She raised her weapon and let out a sigh
She opened her mouth with something to say

You may get me, this may be the day
But you will have a fleshly price to pay
So, go ahead and take a chance,
I'm ready for this final dance

FOREVER IS TOO SMALL

You make forever seem too small
Almost like it's nothing at all
Your eyes hold the promise of a story untold
Of a love that is reckless, wild and bold
An unwavering gaze that sets me ablaze
I want to fall asleep in your arms when the stars wink
      in the sky
And the moon is bright and high
Then, wake up slowly next to you
Choosing to create the moment anew
That forever more will be my before
Marking time as memories sometimes do

IT WAS IN YOU ALL ALONG

You always had the power
Even though you didn't know it
Until the last hour
It was in you all along
And even though you thought so, you didn't get it
      wrong
Each step of this journey brought you to this moment,
      this place
Each step brought you to mercy and grace
There was one step forward and two steps to the side
Forward, backward, a wild ride
And in the end we get to go home not with a click of
      our heels and relief
But by God's grace and our belief

MY GARMENT OF SHAME

My unsureties are the pockets that I fill with fear
I carry them with me when I go there and here
Each one different and the same
Each one wild unable to be tamed
The garment with these pockets is made up of shame
Made of secrets, lies, unmet longing and desires
Woven together in an attempt to conspire
My cooperation is all that's required
To keep this garment on

THE BEGINNING

A passionate kiss in the rain
A look that doesn't need to be explained
Falling asleep when the moon is high
Listening for your relaxed sigh
In your arms, within your embrace
The kisses that you softly place
Noticing the big and small, the subtle and bold
This story that is starting to unfold
This is my heart that you gently hold

THE BATTLE

If I live through this day, will I be prepared for the
        dangerous ones yet to be?
In this battle I will meet someone I have never
        known; I think that person is me
As I prepare for what's to come I feel my
        courage wane
I hear all the doubts and fears, whispered by
        my shame
"Not this time!" I shout, as I turn to fight
And I battle the worst in myself, my dark knight
There is give and take, thrust and parry, it's anybody's
        game
The sword of truth cuts through it all... the lies,
        delusions and blame
Leaving me to die or rise up like a Phoenix from the
        flame
I catch my breath and look up and see
Others who have fought like me
Survivors walk on the road, battle-scarred and worn
This is where their dignity and self-worth were born
Weary but with a quiet satisfaction, even though the
        cost was great
It was worth the toll to rid themselves of their
        loathing and their hate

LOOKING FOR THE BEGINNING

I know how it ends, of course I do
I forgot how it began.
It starts so slowly, you don't really understand
Then one day you find yourself nowhere
        you want to be
And you look for the beginning, that moment,
        and you try and see
What went wrong and what was right?
What do you regret? What do you fight?
It seems if I could find the invisible thread
I could unravel this terrible mess
I face the unraveling with some dread
And the problem I begin to address...
And look for the elusive answer so that
        I can mend
And start working my way back from the end

DANCE WITH ME

When I need it the most, that's when I am the hardest
    to love
When I am angry, mean, and dark like the thunder
    clouds above
That's when I desperately want someone to hold me
    in spite of all my pain
Someone who understands all that I can't explain
A champion to pull me back from the edge
A friend who will dance with me along the ledge
A confidant who hears my silent scream
And wakes me from the nightmare dream
And sees a bit of hope for me when I am at my end
Who will remind me that relationships, hearts and
    souls mend
I am more than this moment in time, I am more than
    my pain
I will go on, I'll live my life and I will be ok again

SCARED...
BUT I AM NOT AFRAID

I'm not afraid of dying, we all meet death
      in the end
If I've done it right, I'll embrace death like a long-
      awaited friend
Living is what scares me, I want a life that is full of
      purpose
I don't want to merely wander through all my days
      and barely scratch the surface
I want to create something profound, love fierce
      and deep
I want to stand for those who can't, holding
      no life cheap
I want to stand in my convictions even if my
      legs quake
Speak my truth, from my heart, even if my
      voice shakes
I want to make a difference even if it's only in some
      small way
Give someone peace of mind at the end of their long
      hard day
I want to use up all my talents, till I'm wrung out and
      there is nothing left to give
This is why I find I'm scared to live
I want to be willing to sacrifice, mark the debt paid
I wake up every morning scared... but, I am not afraid

MONSTER OF MY HEART

Just because the monsters are invisible doesn't mean
        their claws are not sharp
Their claws and teeth can pierce your heart
They stalk me with unrelenting need
Using all that they have to succeed
They want to take all I love away
They feed off my pain and sadness each day
They are made up of my fears and shame
They creep along beside me, whispering my blame
Should have, would have, could have, are the words
        they love to use
It's my mind and soul that they want to abuse
Trying to take small pieces
Away
Till nothing's left... and they go away

THIS IS YOUR WARNING

Addiction, I've devoured Demons far
     greater than you
They got everything they deserved,
     all that they were due
So as you raise your craggy head,
     and hiss your deadly breath
Take a moment and contemplate your death
I promise it won't be pretty or fast
I'll happily make the pain last and last
You are done, and you might as well leave
Your lies hold no more sway with me,
     I no longer believe
Your reign of terror is done,
     your dominion has been revoked
So you better leave before I am provoked
I am giving you your warning
You better leave before your momma needs to
     start mourning
I'm taking back my life today
I'm turning my back on you and walking away

THE MERMAID AND THE BOY

The mermaid whispered in his ear.
     She spoke of many things
Of tears and fears and dancers feet and the
     length of angels wings
Why a heart gets hurt and the song a Siren sings
The boy looked into her luminous eyes
He loved her then and there
He never gave a second thought to the fact
     he needed air
He let her wrap her arms around and take
     him to the deep
All the while she promised him a peaceful
     dreamless sleep
Come with me, don't worry, or fret
All your problems and pain you'll forget
He closed his eyes and slipped away, a smile on his
     parted lips
His one and only declaration of love,
     through them barely slips
The mermaid did what mermaids do,
     she felt no regret
For a life cut short, and love's only kiss, and a boy
     she barely met

UNSHED TEARS

I thought the stars were in the sky,
Then I found them in your eyes...
I took a look closer still and saw all your pain
      and fears,
And that the stars in your eyes were really
      unshed tears...
Your pain could fill an ocean
I want to give you my devotion
And get a chance at happiness
I will weather this storm,
You said without darkness the stars can't shine
I long to catch your tears and make you mine
Let me catch your tears
Quell all of your fears,
And hold you till this storm is done
Till once again you feel the sun

INVISIBLE PRISON

We carry our prisons with us, invisible
      chains and bars
Made up of all the shame and pain that is ours
It keeps us from all we are meant to do, and be
It keeps us from our greatness and keeps us
      from being free
It is the walk alone in this world of many
Searching for love and understanding
      from some or any
It's the past we bring with us, that we
      relive everyday
An unasked price that we believe we must pay
It is the belief that our tragedy and sin is too great
No one could love us, so it's our self
      we begin to hate
The secret and tragedy is... we can leave
We can escape this prison as we come to believe
It's as simple and hard as a decision
      made on your knee
To surrender to a power greater than me

SILENT SCREAMS

I've been silently screaming can't you hear?
Desperation, shame, guilt and fear
These are the ties that bind me tight
Madness, fury, and rage are the opponents
      that I fight
Under the watchful judgement eye of authority
The not so silent moral majority
I am more than what you see
I am more than what has happened to me
I am weary from the battle within and without
I am done with this war and all that it is about
I am choosing to walk away
I am choosing to have the final say
The next chapter of my life will be written by me
The choices I make, my decisions to be free

THE MEASURE OF A MAN

How do you read what isn't written?
See what isn't there?
How do you see all the secrets that are written
      in the air?
The thoughts and feelings written on the
      hearts of men
Things that are written without the use of
      paper or pen
It's written in their lives, in their actions,
      loud and clear
It's written in their relationships and in
      all of their tears
It's written in their prayers they speak in fear,
      gratitude, and shame
It's written in their weakness, their devastation, and
      their pain
So measure the man, make the mark of him true
Learn to read what isn't written, learn to see what's
      hidden from view

MY MUSICIAN

You paint your pictures on the silence
An artist of the air
Creating emotions and moving people letting them
        leave behind their cares
Your sound creates a feeling, a story we all share
It brings us together for a moment, a memory
            that lives on
This painting
This artistry,
These notes,
This song

LET THE THUNDER ROLL

Dark clouds filled the sky
I raised my arms and let loose a cry
Let the thunder roll
The wind circled round me
The storm tried to confuse and confound me
Let the thunder roll
I screamed my rage and shook my fist
Stamped my feet, I would turn and twist
Let the thunder roll
I embraced the storm, and I embraced me
I fell down upon my knee
Let the thunder roll
The storm began to dissipate
With it, went my rage and hate
Lord, heal my soul

YOUR MISTRESS

She stole quietly into my life
I didn't even know she was here
She was the shadow at your shoulder whispering
        sweetly in your ear
I was blind to her
As she seduced you away with empty promises to get
        rid of the pain
"You don't have to feel anything, you don't have
        to be sane"
She looked like an angel, but all the devils do
Promising sweet oblivion
To the likes of you
The price of seduction is very high, she whispered
        softly, with a sigh
I want it all
Your integrity, your will, your life...
Forget your children, forget your wife and in the end
        I'll take your soul too
I'll take it all
I'll take you

PLOT TWIST

I played my part, I played it well
I was the plot twist you didn't see coming
As human and failed as all the rest
Even though I thought it was my best
It was also my worst
It was all that I had
And it wasn't enough
It makes me sad
Because all I can think of is the what if's...
What if I had done more or less
What if I had understood all that I saw
What if I had walked away and not tried to
       fix it all?
None of that matters in the end
Because after all of this I lost my friend

LOVE'S QUESTIONS

When we kiss, can you feel the storm
      beneath my skin?
Can you feel the whispers of the universe, and the
      secrets placed within?
Can you taste the stars on my lips as they bathe me in
      their light?
Or hear the moon as it softly says... goodnight?
Does the heat of my passion ignite the flames
      of your desire?
Does it wrap you in a thousand tongues of fire?
Does it make you want to kiss me and feel
      the storm rage through the night?
Do you want to embrace me in the darkness
      and hold me really tight?

LEAVE THE WORLD BETTER

I see humans but no humanity
Just reality and a little insanity
Where is compassion, love, and grace?
What happened to the human race?
They want, and need, and desire
Get more, get it all, you must acquire
Me first, then you, if I'm not too busy
Go here, then there, till your head's
        spinning and dizzy
Can't they see what's right in front of their eyes?
Getting more isn't the prize
Giving is our privilege, our chance to
        make a difference
Loving each other helps us go the distance
It's time for us to see, to open our eyes
It's time for us to be, take a moment and realize
We are in this together
Not one of us is more, or better
None of us will get out alive
None of us this life will survive
So give up on your quest for status and things
See what looking outward brings
Give up your entitlement, addictions, and rage
It's time to turn that ugly page
Stop trying to settle the score
Try to leave the world better than you found it, and
        people better than before

MY DANCE WITH A DEMON

The demon asked me to dance
And really I didn't have a chance
He recognized himself in me
We mirrored each other perfectly
I drank deeply of his sin
Sure I could change him from within
I became drunk with power and control
Bargained away precious parts of my soul
In the end it was clear to see
The only thing I changed was me

LIFE CAN BE LIKE THAT

No one expects an angel to set the world on fire, just
        to watch it burn
But life can be like that, we learn
Full of surprises, not fair, or right
Answers sometimes hidden, sometimes in
        plain sight
Love, although truly earned, may not be returned
Sometimes, walking away is the price we
        have to pay
Home can be a broken place
Infinity can be a small space
And angels might light the fire that will
        show us the way
To all of our dismay

DISTANCE BETWEEN US

When we feel a longing
And want belonging
We seek a connection with another
The distance between us is not because of
　　　　time or space
But the distance of understanding between us,
　　　　that takes place
If I can understand what you think, or the emotions
　　　　that you feel
That's one step closer that I can take to heal

A LITTLE TOO REAL

She looked like a normal girl
The kind whose hair was brown with curls
She held a secret within, it's true
She was very different than me or you
She believed in long kisses, and fairy tales,
Unicorns, and dragon scales
That people were basically good, true love
        never dies
And warriors and heroes have the saddest eyes
In a terribly fake world she was a little too real
Which explains all of the pain she could feel
And why she desperately loved the moon and rain
Why people questioned if she was sane

A BEAUTIFUL NIGHTMARE

I was broken, but beautifully sewn
He was a king, made only of frosty white bone
Our love was born of the darkest night
Celebrated with Halloween fright
You'll find us under the stars side by side
A love like ours you cannot hide
It is something amazing to see
A beautiful nightmare meant to be

MY LOVER THE MOON

The moon has two sides, one dark and one light
One that he keeps hidden and one we can see at night
He plays with stars and moves the sea
Inspires us so effortlessly
He marches east to west
He lingers even though he's done
Hoping to catch a glimpse of his lover the sun

LIVE OUT LOUD

Shame tells me where I start and end
It tells me that it's my friend
It tells me what to do and say
It tells me it's a small price to pay
Satan knows my name but he calls me
        by my shame
He wants me to listen to the pain
He wants me to believe,
All he wants is to deceive
Then one day I'm done
I hear about the Son
He knows about my shame and yet he calls to
        me by name
All he wants from me is love
I will praise my God above
I want to live my life out loud, live it proud
Proud to be a daughter of the King

THE QUIET IS SO LOUD

Lying alone in the dark
I awake with a start
I listen to see if there is a sound
The quiet is so loud
I look to the side of the bed where you should be
Tears fill my eyes and my heart breaks anew
As the pictures of our life together start to
       fill my head
My eyes and arms aching for you
I wasn't complete
I could never compete
With the seduction of escape

LOVE IS RIGHT

The lies and delusion create mass confusion
I long for a place I've never been
Where the hero is reckless and bold
Acting despite his fear
In a way he knows is right
Choosing the path even though it's hard
A place where I can fight beside him and know he has
      my back
And at the end of our journey we would hold each
      other tight
Long into the night
Knowing we will face it all again
And that it's worth the risk, and it's worth
      the fight
And even when we lose we win because love
      is right

DARK KNIGHT

He came to me on bended knee
In black armor for all to see
Cloaked in darkness and mystery
With a violent and painful history
He pledged his sword and his shield
Saying his protection would never yield
He pledged his soul and his heart
Saying only his death would make us part
He said the things I longed to hear
You'll be safe and I'll cherish you dear
But I knew his biggest battle was yet to come
And to this enemy most will succumb
A great and powerful demon of old
Whose lies and temptations were strong and bold
So I sent him off to war to battle for his life and soul
Knowing full well the cost and the toll
To face all the darkness, fear and shame
And battle himself, and all the pain
This could be the battle that wins the war
That marks his life forever more
As the defining moment, that he came to know
He was the master of his fate, and he defeated his foe

EVERY FEELING

Let the storm rage
I need to feel it all
Every feeling, every one, the big and small
Let it course through me
Till I know it through and through
Knowing it as intimately as two lovers do
Let me dance with it and feel the give and take
Seeing all the missed steps and the mistakes
And when I know the storm and I've danced
       the pain away
Let me say goodbye and thank you
And let it go away

I LONG FOR CONNECTION

I'm on the outside looking in
I want to be part of... but I don't know
        where to begin
Sometimes I dress up in their fancy clothes
I'll even watch their TV shows
The more like them I try to be
I'm more outside, it seems to me
I use the irrelevant words and phrases
        that they say
"How is the weather?" And "have a nice day"
This just shows me what is painfully true
I can never really be like you
I crave understanding as deep as the ocean
Conversations with true emotions
Someone who can see my battered soul and
        not turn away
But invites me in, and wants me to stay

THE TIME BETWEEN

It's the time between the lightning flash and
The thunder's crash
When you hold your breath in expectation
The time between one heartbeat and the next
       listening and feeling the exaltation
The time between the
First kiss and the next where we wait
       with anticipation
That's where we meet our hearts desire
And that's where we ignite passion's fire
That's where love begins anew
That is where I wait for you

BASKET OF LIES

I saw an old stooped man with a basket walking on
    the road
I started to walk beside him and asked if I could help
    with his load
He stopped walking and looked at me with a frown
And slowly put his heavy basket down
He looked off in the distance, then into my eye
Then he took out a red handkerchief as he
    started to cry
He sniffed, and dabbed, and he put the
    handkerchief away
And then slowly opened his mouth with
    something to say
This basket is mine
I have to carry it till the end of time
It's full of all the lies I've told
From the small little white to the blatant and bold
It's heavy, and burdensome and I wish I could
    put it down
And then I remember this is nothing compared to the
    damage they've done, he said with a frown
I would like to give you a piece of advice
So you can avoid having to pay this high price
The truth no matter how ugly and hard
    will set you free
And a lie is always wrong no matter how easy

So guard the truth, speak it even if you think people
        will be upset
Because, there is nothing that is worth the high
        price of regret
With that the old man picked up the basket of lies
Looked one more time deep in my eyes
Shifted his heavy load and turned and walked
        down the road

THE DEMON ME

I do beautiful and terrible things
I'm a demon with beautiful wings
I'll love you and hurt you in equal part
Steal your breath and your heart
Teach you to see the impossible and how to fly,
Make you laugh maniacally, and then start to cry
It is dangerous to love me,
          you will never be the same
When I leave, you will wish I never came
You'll long for the days before
When you didn't long for anything more
Than what you had and what you could see
Before you met the demon me

I BLAME THE MOON

I blame the moon
I lost myself in those kisses
In the urgent need for you
I lost my sense of time and place
All the world stopped
And I noticed how you made me feel
I noticed I had begun to heal
I noticed that my heart had begun to beat again
And I noticed that I forgot to be afraid, even if it was
        just for a minute
I started looking out and stopped looking in
There was a world where love didn't ask too much
And I could believe in it again
Where the truth was told and promises kept
And it was safe to breathe again

MY SILENCE SPEAKS

My silence speaks a thousand words
My tears hold all my pain,
How could I have been so dumb?
Can I ever trust again?
Can I believe that love won't hurt?
That love won't ask me to pay a price?
That it won't demand my very soul
An ultimate sacrifice?

LOVE ME FIERCELY

Embrace my storms and darkness,
    light my soul afire
Dance with me in the flames of my desire
Love me fiercely or not at all
Rise to my love, don't merely fall
Kiss me till you feel the thunder under my skin
Teach me the cypher that reveals your heart's
    secrets within
Sing to me your soul's song,
The one with no words,
    that you can never get wrong
Keep me safe and protected all the night through
So I can go on loving you

TIME TO PLAY, TIME TO PRAY

When my monsters and demons come out to play
That's when you should start to pray
Call out for your soul's redemption
Scream out your fear and apprehension
Run like you're being chased by the hounds of hell
And you have just heard your death's knell
You see, I keep the monsters and demons
      locked up sure
Until you push me past what I can endure
Then I loose them for all to see
And let them feed hungrily
They are my ultimate solution
As they seek to give me my retribution

PRISON STEW

Humpy dumpty was on the rack
They broke his shell with a thunderous crack
And all of the inmates and the hangman too
Were glad for the break from prison stew

A SCARY BEAUTIFUL DANCE

I'm scared of this beautiful dance
It requires a vulnerable me
A letting go, a submission,
A chance to get hurt again.
I want to do it...
And it could be the last thing I ever do...
This thing, this loving you.
And, I know that I am brave.
I know that I should allow trust to be earned.
I know that you're a good man.
So, as I hand you a knife and the map of my soul
Be gentle, and trustworthy...
This could be the last thing I do, this loving you...

REAL, BUT NOT TRUE

My feelings are real, but not true
They tell me lies I want to believe
They are weapons meant to deceive
To keep me off balance and always unsure
Alone, frightened, slightly insane, there is a
      slight allure
To leave behind all the work, the real,
      the unknown
And embrace the pain
You see, it tells me where I start and where I end,
It tells me that it's my friend
And without it I don't know what to do
With these feelings that are real, but not true

CLOAKED IN DARKNESS, ON MY OWN

You saw me cloaked in darkness
Breathing loneliness
Standing on the edge
Always apart not a part of
Your hand touched mine and you brought me to the
      here and now
But the darkness came too
It followed everywhere sometimes just out of sight
      and then you left
And now it creeps closer everyday
Sometimes threatening to steal me away
There is no one to bring me back now,
      I'm on my own

THE RAIN BROUGHT
THOUGHTS OF YOU

I woke up to the sound of rain and it brought
       thoughts of you
The press of your lips against my neck
The sound of our laughter at a joke only we get
The look in your eyes as I catch them from
       across a room
The fiery passion that will consume
The passing of time in the blink of an eye
The hug that elicits a contented sigh
The rain brought these thoughts with it today
Along with the raindrops and a sky of grey

MY JOURNEY

When I start to feel regret
It's only because I forget
How far and through what I have survived
And every last time, even when I wasn't sure,
      I made it out alive
My character was forged in the flames and
      heat of each trial
It was shaped with each step taken, mile after mile
My strength and courage were a choice,
      not chance
They didn't happen by circumstance
I will use these lessons to motivate me to
      do my best
So I will pass each and every test
I'll make the changes, not an excuse
Self-esteem not self-pity is what I'll choose
And even if this is the hardest lesson yet
I'll get through it you can bet

DANCING ON THE EDGE

She dances at the edge of a cliff, not caring that she
    could fall
She spins and leaps and stamps her feet, not thinking
    about it at all
People think she's crazy, she must not care
    if she dies,
She smiles at them with a wicked grin, and simply
    shakes her head and sighs
You see she knows a truth,
    a secret some would say
All of us are going to die,
    we just don't know on which day
Living, on the other hand, that's something only a few
    people do,
Most are simply not dying each and every day their
    whole lives through
They're scared or in pain or so full of their shame,
    they won't take a chance
To climb the mountain and hear its song, and walk to
    the edge and dance

RAGE IS BORN

My rage was born the moment you didn't
      believe me
It grew and flourished each time you deceived me
And when you told me to pretend it didn't happen
      when we both know it did
That's when I learned I had to keep my
      feelings hid
When you didn't come to my defense,
And let the unspeakable commence
I learned about fear, dread, and hate
I learned I better go along, and accommodate
I found I had strength to endure, persist,
      and prevail
How to survive and all that entailed
I've learned those lessons well, to my very core
Today's the day I will say...
Not anymore
I was worth protecting, and believing and
      what's more
I was so worth fighting for

BEAUTIFUL

You call me beautiful like it's my name
Ignite my desire and fan the flame
You count each star with kisses placed just so
A spiraling, winding, invisible row
Your fingers trace a gentle path along my face
Your arms hold me in a reassuring embrace
You speak your words to my soul burning it
      like a brand
You tangle your fingers in my hair wrapping the curls
      in your hand
I believe you when you call me beautiful like
      it's my name
This wild reckless beauty you have tamed

DON'T ANSWER HIS CALL

The devil comes disguised as everything you have
        ever been wanting
Whispering, calling, telling bold lies, and taunting
Asking questions you know the answer to, making
        you doubt what you know to be true
Planting envy, sowing unrest
Telling you this pathetic attempt is really
        your best
It's ok to stop, it's ok to lay it all down because your
        life is unfair
Go ahead embrace your despair
The devil comes, looking for your soul
Taking it for his own is his goal
He'll come trying to get it all
Just don't answer when he comes to call

LITTLE GIRL

My little girl, my little me
She is naive and trusting you see
She wants to do good
She wants to do right
She is afraid she is too little
She is afraid she's not right
She is afraid she is too much
She wants to be bright
She is vulnerable
She is sweet
She is with me always
She is me

HUBRIS

You made me your God and worshiped
     at my altar
It could never last I'm not perfect I will falter
I just wanted to love you and build a life
You wanted a savior not a wife
It's no surprise that I couldn't make you whole
I couldn't make you better or heal your soul
In my arrogance and pride I thought I could
I thought maybe I was really that good
I tried to be what you thought you would need
In the end there was no way to succeed
This hubris is my sin for sure
Broken is my only cure

GIRL WITH THE FATHOMLESS EYES

I saw a little girl on the side of the road
Beside her on the ground was a very large load
She was hard to look at, she was hard to see
She seems somehow familiar to me
She looked at me with fathomless eyes
And that look, I did despise
She filled me with loathing she filled me
            with dread
I wanted to turn, but I approached her instead
Who are you!? I asked, full of apprehension
I'm everything and nothing she said with intention
I am the truth I am the lie
I am the whole story she breathed a sigh
I am the victim and the villain too
Everything you want and believe you were due
All of the ugliness on your worst day
A reminder of the price you must pay...
I'm all that you must embrace
Your shame, disappointments and your disgrace
"Why?" I asked, trembling in fear
She asked "Are you sure you want to hear?"
I found myself nodding yes
Even through my distress
She gave me a look that made me weak
She opened her mouth and she started to speak
When you were busy and on the go.
I'm the one who ran the show

When you were angry and felt like a fool
I reached in this bag and took out a tool
You left me in charge when you wanted to play
Or when life was hard and you wanted to
     just go away
When you were angry, hurt, or sad
When you acted out, or were mean or bad
I own it all, every memory, action, and feeling
And you must embrace me if you want
     to start healing
I looked at her stunned and I started to cry
As she looked at me with her fathomless eyes
This is me by another name
This is the embodiment that causes me
     guilt and shame
My ugliest truth, my despicable me
All of this I'm beginning to see
Can I love her? Forgive her? Treat her right?
Can I embrace her? Can I give up this fight?
I can be willing at least for today
To be here and not run away...
I can sit and talk for a bit
Embrace her a moment while we sit
Someday maybe I can learn to hold her tight
Look at her and treat her right
Cherish all that she is and has done
The lessons learned and the healing begun

LET ME...

Let me feel the thunder let me feel the waves
Let me feel the disappointment let me feel the rage
Let me dance with it like it's my lover till I know it
      through and through
Put it to the test until I know that it is true
Let me scream, vilify, and rave
Let me rend my clothes, and tear my hair, lay within
      my grave
Let me purge my soul, and leave this all behind
Then come back to it anew
Then when I am done let me be through

WHO IS WILLING?

I long for a love not afraid of my dark
Who can hold the angry, wild riot of my heart
Who won't run from the ruins of my soul
And knows how to survive its frosty cold
Willing to live at the edge of light
Where darkness begets an endless night
The one who can tame my demons and put them into
       a deep slumber
That's the one for whom I hunger

KISS ME

Wrap me in a blue velvet blanket trimmed
       with stars
Tell me a sweet story of the love that is ours
Trace intricate patterns on my bare skin
Leaving a fiery trail where your fingers have been
Kiss me deeply, and let me drink you in
The kiss that lets me love again

JUDGE AND JURY

You left me
It was your job to protect me
I was yours to hold and keep
Instead he got me, the monster from the deep
That was where my life was torn
That was where my unending rage was born
Rage grew until it consumed me
Took over, and with my shame it assumed me
And now I want the world to pay
I want the world to burn, I want him to pray
I want to be the judge and the jury
I want him to quiver with fear and worry
So he will know what it's like to feel
His soul ripped away with no chance for appeal
And let him listen to his victims' unending screams,
      with every breath
As he begs for release and sweetly elusive death

MONSTERS I KEEP

How do I put to sleep,
All the monsters that I keep
And wipe away my salty tears
Chase away all my fears
I'm so tired of the endless battle I am trying to win
In this horrific war I have found myself in
It's me against the world at large
That's my ego leading the charge
It's me against my family and friends
That's my shame that has no end
It's me against myself and I
"No one wins" is that battle cry
It's me against my God above
I am not worthy of His love
Do I count it a victory because I survive,
Because I made it through once more alive?
Is there something more, another way to be
A healthier, wiser and happier me
Oh how do I put these monsters to sleep
So at the end of the battle my soul I can keep?

STORM CHASER

You must be a storm chaser, not afraid of the chaos,
    turmoil, and rage
The type who wants to see what will happen so, you
    let the monster out of his cage
You pit yourself against him again and again
Laughing at the battle even if you don't win
The monster is ancient, patient, and reeks of death
He waits, biding his time, to steal your last breath
Determination, force of will, and intention are not
    enough
You can't out-monster the monster, you can't be that
    tough
The battle within is the one that will win this war
The ultimate way to settle this score
And beat this monster, watch him fall
As you walk away victorious, once and for all
The monster back in his cage
You the master of chaos, turmoil, and rage

DARK DELIGHT

A passion as dark as a moonless sky
Fills my heart and makes me sigh
My pulse begins to race beneath my skin
Creating a chaos deep within
I taste your name as it so effortlessly slips
From between my parted lips
And all the creatures of the night
Stop, and take notice of my delight

A LIFE SUSPENDED

A life suspended until I could fix what was wrong
Always apart wanting to belong
Slowly I began one moment at a time
Breathing, thinking, and laughing
And as those moments added up
I found that I was living my life
With peace, joy, and love

IN THE END

I tried and I cried
And in the end
It didn't matter
Your lies were told
Blatant and bold
The victim was my heart and soul
Don't act surprised at the look in my eyes
Or my silence as I walk away

OUR DEMONS DANCE

Your demon cries out to mine
And a chorus of shivers climbs my spine
They recognize each other you see
The demons that live in you and me
Anticipation and tension start to dance
A passionate tango of romance
The madness will try to consume
As we dance with our demons in the full
   light of the moon

I AM BRAVE

I'm not a damsel in distress
I don't need to be saved
I am a heroine, I am brave
I know that I can do what it takes to
      get the job done
I can fight the fight till the battle's won
I can slay the dragon and finish the quest
But, when it's over and I am through
Oh then, what will I do?
You see, I was doing it all for you...

MY SECRET PLACE

That space between seconds
Is where I think of you
A space beyond time where we share what is true
Our souls remembering each other
A place we kiss one another
A place where moments aren't counted and hours
Fall away
Where there is no yesterday or tomorrow,
        but only today
This is the place where I think of you

A STORY NEVER TOLD

A story that has never been told
Of warriors both beautiful and bold
Fighting for the greater good
Making hard choices when they should
Putting their lives out on the line
Looking death right in the face
Knowing any moment they may leave this place
Ready to make a sacrifice for the greater good
Calling to God for their protection
He answers with the resurrection

THE QUESTION

This is the question that your soul would ask if it
    could speak
Do I have what it takes? Am I powerful or am I weak?
The answer comes from you inside
It really is what you decide
No one else has a say
If you have what it takes tomorrow and today
Not your coach
Not your dad
Not your teacher
Not your happy or your sad
Not your mom
Not your preacher
Or some person down the street
Not one person that you meet
Not society at large
Or some imaginary person in charge
You decide if you have what it takes
It is your decision alone to make
Will you rise to the challenge, and take your place
    among men
Will you claim your birthright, and declare it from
    now till then
Stand tall, steadfast, and proud
And say it finally out loud
As loud as you can
I... I am a MAN

AWAY

How I long to be
Away from everything that is me
All the regret and the shame
All the confusion and the pain
I want to soar with an eagle free
Just to be away from me

ONE MORE TIME

I want magic to exist
So one more time I could feel your kiss
And hear your voice call my name
Feel the love that you proclaim
I would have time bend
So that last moment would never end
In to your eyes I would stare
If there was magic in the air

REBEL

I am the storm. They say my quarrel is with the sky
My rebellion started with the simple question "why?"
And continued with standing for those who
      no longer could,
Against those who knew better, or at
      least they should
I came into this world screaming and bloody, is it a
      surprise that I am willing to leave it
      the same way?

I will not back down, or conform, if there is a price I
      will gladly pay
I am sorry if I make you uncomfortable with my
      questions and my truth
Blame it on the way I was raised, my character,
      or my youth
You see, I don't need your approval, I am no longer
      following the rules
I won't keep your secrets, that's a test for other fools
I came to life for this rebellion, you can taste it
      on my lips
My courage and desire never waiver, they never slip
I am a wild thing of the night, I run fast and free
You can glorify or vilify, but, don't ignore me
My halo is made of carrion birds waiting for my fall
They want my eyes, hair, and flesh, they want it all
If this is my last day, then it is a good day to die

Cause' we will go together cheek to cheek and
       eye to eye
In the end my body is just a shell,
But, my soul... My soul is your escort to hell

PUPPET MASTERS

I'm not what you want, I am all that you desire
I'm nothing you need, I am everything you require
Sweet oblivion, escape, and no more pain are the lies
    that I have sold you
Once you've tasted my lies you'll believe
    all that I've told you
The give and take between us is just an illusion
You give and I take that's the unspoken collusion
You are like a puppet who dances when I
    pull the strings
I am the puppet master that your misery brings
You hate me and long for me in equal parts,
    it's true
I just laugh knowing there is nothing you won't do
I say "jump" you say "how high?"
You say "I quit, I'm leaving you"
I say "go ahead and try"

WILD CREATURE

They say the heart's a wild creature that's why we
        keep it in a cage
It's capable of deep abiding love and
        unbridled rage
It longingly calls out, sometimes so soft you
        strain to hear
Other times it's loud, like thunder to your ear
The calling, searching, for another — it seems one
        half of a whole
Always looking, longing, and seeking another soul

THE BARD

Sounds become notes, one by one
The notes a melody, and the song has begun
You bring it forth like an elemental magic, and give it
     the breath of life
Then hold it like your lover while you dance on the
     edge of a knife
You whirl us to the heights of joy, lead us to the
     depths of our despair
Remind us of the things we know and establish how
     much we care
When we've felt each emotion, seen each memory
     through to the end
You bring us back to ourselves, and the music, and
     leave us wanting to hear it again

ANYONE CAN BE A HERO

A hero can be anyone its true
It could be me, it could be you
We only have to be willing to do what
      others won't
To see the things that others don't
Step forward when someone else steps back
Defend the fallen, pick up the slack
Be willing to say
Enough is enough, not on my watch, not today
I'm willing to do what's hard and if there is a price, I
      will gladly pay
I will speak for the silent
I will defend the weak
I will comfort those who need it and wipe a tear from
      their cheek
A hero can be anyone its true...
What are you willing to do?

THE GIFT I RECEIVED

You gave me darkness and that's a gift too
It allowed me to see the moon and the stars and learn
      to dance in their light
You gave me rain and I learned to hear the music that
      it made
So, whenever I danced I always had a tune
You gave me indifference and that gift was
      harder to see...
But, that was the gift of knowing me

MY NORMAL NOW

The tears dried up and went away
I locked them up tight to keep my feelings at bay
Then my world turned upside down, I fell through the
      rabbit hole
Nothing was the same and for the answers I had to
      search my soul
The tears came back with a vengeance it seems
I'll cry for love, and pain, and lost dreams
I can't say I like it
This aching, feeling, vulnerable me
Apparently this is my normal now
This is how I'll be

AN INVISIBLE WALL

All the lies I couldn't bear
Are hanging between us in the air
An invisible wall impossible to scale
I'm on one side and you're on the other
Both of us wanting each other and unable
        to find a way
I never thought that it would end, this life I built with
        my friend
But I can't scale an invisible wall
I can't solve this impossible maze
I can't hear a silent call
Or see through all of this murky haze

THE ILLUSIONS WE BELIEVE

The illusion that we believed
Is that we had enough time, we were deceived
We thought that we could say I love you and kiss
      goodnight
We could tell someone how we really felt and hold on
      to them really tight
Time would be on our side
We thought in our pride
Because we want to believe that this will
      never end
That we have time for anger and regret
We have time for grudges and to be upset
That's the illusion don't you see
We just had love
You and me

DIGNITY IS BORN

I want a pound of flesh and holy retribution
I'm not looking for any absolution
Bring him to his knees
Ignoring all of his pleas
There is no atonement to be had
For a life and a man, so sick and sad
He died before the toll could be exacted
Before the confession could be extracted
And now I am left unfulfilled and wanting more
With no way to settle the score
No way to engage
I am left with an impotent rage
I shake my fist, scream out in the night
I constantly look for a fight
With nothing on the outside I turn the battle in
Much to my chagrin
It's me against myself and I
And all the terrible, horrible lies
A win is a loss in this equation
No victor on this occasion
No celebration song to be sung
No bright and colorful banners to be hung
And then some pieces fall in place
And there I'm met with God's grace
There a quiet dignity is born
An unlikely mantle worn
As dear as a medal made of gold

Given to the heroes of old
I take satisfaction in God above
And live my life in peace, joy and love

PLAIN AND SIMPLE

The silver light of the moon plays softly
    with my hair
The stars leave me breathless and
I see you sitting there
I lean toward you for a kiss and feel your heart beat
    against my hand
Then you kiss me and I begin to understand
That this is love
Plain and simple it's true
Love for me is you

THIS MASK

It's the first thing on and the last thing
       off every day
This mask that keeps the world at bay
The barrier between the people and me
Keeping me safe and distant is the key
It's how I bear the pain
In part what keeps me sane
This mask between the world and me

LOVE CAN CUT DEEP

Just because you see me strong,
Doesn't mean that nothing's wrong
A smile can hide a thousand tears
My silence cloaks a thousand fears
Love can cut deeper than a razor blade
And wound my soul, the ultimate price paid

I want to know why
Why the lies
Why the escape
Why I wasn't worth the truth

A SMALL GIRL

Little Miss Muffet sat on her tuffet all
        proper and prim
An evil man
Pulled up in a van
And tried to lure her in

Come here little girl... I have candy that's sweet
And if you get in I'll give you a treat

Miss Muffet was much more than she seemed
She was made of the nightmares you dreamed

Men like him she ate for dinner and dessert
Men like him she liked to hurt

So in the van she went with a smile
They didn't get down the road quite a mile
When out of the van Miss Muffet came
No sign of the man
No one to blame
Because she was just a small girl it couldn't be her
        they knew
Well, everyone except for you

SWEET ECHO

When you kiss me the world falls away
And a depth of emotion it does convey
And all the things that seem so important take their
        place at the back of my mind
The things that truly matter I find
As you kiss me the whisper of sweet nothings said
Echo sweetly in my head
When you move my hair to kiss my neck or whisper
        in my ear
When you hold me and I know no fear
And for a moment I don't have to be strong
And to you that isn't wrong
These are important to me
These things I cherish... don't you see?

MONSTERS UNDER MY BED

When I was young I was afraid of the dark and
    monsters under my bed
Now I know that the monsters are living
    inside my head
They travel with me wherever I may go
Whispering to me endlessly
Torturing me just so
I'm not unique or special
We all have them you see
The difference is in the details
And that this one lives in me

NIGHT WINDS LULLABY

Night wind whispers a lullaby
While we linger under the dark night sky
Stars call to us and say goodnight
Moon bathes us with his golden light
I see you in silhouette
This night, this moment, I won't forget
It's etched on my heart you see
So I'll have it for eternity

THE STORY YOU TELL

In the small quiet hours of the night
When you lie awake and your eyes burn bright
And hope and desperation are all you can smell
What is the story that you tell?
Is it of the hero that's battle worn?
Weary of the fight from which he was born
Striving to do whatever it takes
Ready to defend what's his, no matter how high
      the stakes
Or, is it the story of a person who is not
      good enough
Who isn't at all sinewy, brave or tough
Is he full of self-doubt, dread and, fear
Too scared to do the hard work, to save all that
      he holds dear
The secret is they are one and the same
The only difference is their shame
One lets shame be the king reigning with dominion
      over all that he sees
Allowing it to do whatever he please
The other has fought shame, not sure if he can win in
      the end
He counts shame as a wary friend

THE STORY SOLD

The lie was bold
The story was sold
Bought, even though the price was too high
It cost trust, self-esteem, and respect
All for the promise of love...
It was a lie
Betrayal, hurt, sacrifice, and in the end the
        ultimate price
It kept you from loving me
Having the life that you deserve
It stole your peace, joy, and happiness
The only hope now comes from God above
So down on your knees you beg him... "please... let me
        come home"
And you can't believe that He would love you
You can't believe he never left you
That the power to come home... you've always had

MY HEART

You awakened the long-sleeping monster in my
chest...
It shakes its head and roars as it rises from its
long and troubled rest
The secret thrill and fear are both felt in equal part
As it comes alive after so long, my cold and dormant
heart
It aches with a ravenous hunger
As it ascends from its long dreamless slumber
It looks to feed upon the bold desire that
you ignite
Sate itself in your wild passion and delight
And take its place once again among the living,
claiming dominion over all that it can see
The ruler of emotions so ecstatic to be free

PERHAPS

Can I talk about my anger and rage... perhaps?
No, we're doing addiction and relapse
Can I talk about my sadness and pain... perhaps?
No, we are doing addiction and relapse
Can I talk about my fear and apprehension... perhaps?
No, we are doing addiction and relapse
Can I talk about the mistakes I made and things I did
  wrong... perhaps?
No, we are doing addiction and relapse
Can I talk about how I feel small and want to
  disappear... perhaps?
No, we are doing addiction and relapse
Can I talk about how lonely I am and how ugly I feel...
  perhaps?
No, we are doing addiction and relapse
Can I talk about anything? The connections I've
  made, the revelations I've had, the hurt and
  the sorrow, the insights, the triumph and joy,
  the regrets, the unspoken promises, the lies,
  rewritten stories, the hope for the future,
  feeling lost, abandoned, the abuse, the secrets
  and lies... perhaps?
No we are doing addiction and relapse
Can I talk about my anger and rage...

ALL HALLOWS' EVE

It was a dark night where even the skeptics believe
It was the night they call All Hallows' Eve
The veil between worlds is stretched mighty thin
Monsters, goblins, and ghouls can get in
They wait for cute children seeking tricks and treats
Hoping that they can get some good tasty eats
So mind your children on that night
They might get more than just a fright

THAT MOMENT

There is an extraordinary moment in the midst of an
      ordinary day
When you suddenly take notice of me, and the
      common world slips away
Time goes by the wayside
And a moment takes a year
And I don't care whether I am there or here
Our eyes lock, your lips find mine
Tongues and arms intertwine
That magic kiss that stops me in my tracks...
Ends and the world comes crashing back

I AM...

I am more than you think
I am a hurricane of emotion
I am a well of self-doubt
I am a shield of protection
I am a soft shoulder of comfort
I am the sympathetic ear of compassion
I am wisdom
I am the consummate fool
I am a temptress
I am strong
I am weak
I am a hopeless romantic
I am a selfish
I am a coward afraid to speak
I am a keeper of words
I am a product of sin
I am redeemed in Christ

ALICE

There once was a hatter who was mad you see
All he liked to drink was tea
He had two friends: a mouse and a hare
And when they annoyed him he would give them a
      glare
One day a strange girl came for tea
Her name was Alice, coincidentally
She did practically everything wrong
She didn't know the unbirthday song
She was looking for the white rabbit,
      who was very late
So she left right after they broke a plate
And never again shall they like to see
Alice the strange girl who came to tea

OUR FEAST

We sit at a banquet laid with stars
This night alone is ours
We feast on passion, and drink our desire
And thrill ourselves as the fates conspire
To send us both our separate ways
With only this memory for the rest of our days

BROKEN PIECES

You slipped between my shadow and soul and found
    my heart
It was no longer whole, but broken into pieces, it had
    come completely apart
You didn't run away and hide
You pushed all my protests aside
And quite methodically set about to put it
    together again
It won't be the same, different but not bad, you said
    with a grin
So using grace, trust, and love for thread, and a needle
    of honesty and hope
Each piece was stitched together one by one
Until you handed it back to me, completely done
It looked a little crooked, tattered and worn
You said that's where my character was born
There were cracks and holes where I was afraid the
    love could spill away
You said that's so more love could sneak in to stay
This act of love was a wonderful token
You made my heart more beautiful for having
    been broken

MORE ME

I thought that you made me more me,
But, you made me who I am
I thought I needed to take care of you
That was part of an unspoken plan
I thought you made me part of the baffling world,
   every time you held my hand
That was just to keep me blind to what
   was going on
A really fast dance to a really bad song

MISTRESS OF THE SHADOWS

Mistress of the shadows makes you want more
She'll dance with your demons and make
     them roar
You'll fall in love, and feel regret
You'll wish that you could forget
Her touch will repulse and thrill you
Her kiss will both stir your passion and kill you
You'll ask yourself why you can't just walk away
And leave her behind without delay
Remember what a beautiful angel the devil
     was before he fell,
And had to walk into Hell

I STILL FEEL

I am ready to move on...
So why do I cry when I hear this song?
I ache in places that I didn't know I had.
Why do I still feel this bad?
I wanted to be worth fighting for
The reason the waves still kiss the shore
The reason the moon looked to the sun as she rose for
      the day and he went to bed
The reason we love our roses red
I wanted to be worth all the hard work
And I know now it can't be for me
You can only do it for you
But I really, really wanted you to...

LIKE ME

When you walk alone among many
The most crowded space can seem empty
Your eyes constantly scan to see if there is anyone
      else who sees
The heartbreak, anguish, fears,
The triumphs, love, accomplishments and tears
The quiet victories
The smallest connections
The furtive glance
If you find another who sees like you and feels the
      anguish of the rain
Who feels like you the depth of other
      peoples' pain
Keep that person close to you they are far
      and few between
The person who can see like you but isn't seen

A LOVE THAT COULDN'T LAST

The night sky was full of the moon and stars
They were ours
They marked the time together that tasted
      so sweet
Like the secret that two lovers keep
Deep kisses that intoxicated the senses like a
      fruity wine
Each one placed along my neck in a fiery line
The time together passed
Too fast
For a love that couldn't last
I look up and count the stars
And remember the love that was ours

RETRIBUTION

I will make trophies of their spines
These hated enemies of mine
And all will come to rue the day
That I exact the price they pay
For all the wrongs they've done to me
Retribution will be my key
I will make them long for this...
Death's embrace and final kiss

ALL OF YOU

Show me all of you, both the light and the dark
I am not afraid of the shadows on your heart
I hunger for your heart's desire
To know what fuels your passion's fire
I want to know the parts you'd rather tuck away
I want to know what you long for and for what
      you pray
I want you to introduce me to your secrets
      deep within
I want to know what feeds your soul
And where your nightmares begin
I want to know your monsters and what
      makes them grin
Where your heart is going and where your
      heart has been
It's easy to love the light but I want the dark too
Because when I love, it will be all of you

A DIFFERENT TRUTH

How was I so blind
Why could I never see
What was staring back at me?
I assigned a different meaning to the truth
      that was so bold
I believed the lie that to me was told
Why didn't I question, push, or prod?
Why didn't I think that this situation was odd?

There's nothing I can say,
No words to convey
The hows and the whys of my thoughts
I know better now
So I do better now
That was the lesson I was taught

A LITTLE BRAVE

I'm sad that you don't want to play
I'm angry that this is all you have to say
I wanted and deserved so much more,
At least as much as I gave
Why can't you be just a little brave
Just say the things that you don't want to say
Tell all the secrets that you have locked away
Step out of the dark and into the light
Get rid of your secrets that are locked up tight

DARKNESS, MY LOVE

Darkness is my new lover
We know each other well
Each of us falling under the other's spell
Darkness lets me see the beauty of the moon
      and the stars
He reminds me every night of the love that is ours
He wraps himself around me till he touches me
      on each side
Until I can see nothing even with my eyes
      open wide
My pulse starts to race, my chest starts to get tight
My lover starts to pull away and I notice that here
      comes the light

THIS IS WHO I HAVE BECOME

Angry is my protective shield
It motivates the weapons I yield
I am chaotic and bold
Not someone to be controlled
Not someone to dismiss and cast aside
I am the one to get the job done
Work a lot no time for fun
Make hard decisions
Hold the line
Stand in the gap
Steel rod for a spine
It's not who I want to be
Oh why is it you cannot see?
This is what I have become, not who I am
I want to be a girl who's soft, a girl who's smart
A girl who's not afraid for her heart

WHO ARE YOU?

When I asked you who you were
You answered but I didn't believe
In my mind you see I could not conceive
That the words you said were not true
But the actions they were the cue
I should have seen what was so plain
My only excuse was the pain
Of seeing you as you

WILD AND FREE

The wild ponies run a race under the
    starry night sky
Chasing the songs of the night wind as it
    whispers and sighs
They smell the thrill of hope and promise with
    each inhalation
They are cheered on by each starry constellation
Hooves pound the ground like a bass drum
Their hearts pound and beat as one
They're fierce and proud
Wild and free
With those ponies I long to be

IF ME, THEN YOU

I always thought that if I worked as
        hard as I could
Then you would learn and do what you should
I thought if I sacrificed just a little more
Then you would finally me adore
I thought if I just showed you what you should do
Then you would want to do it too
I've learned this isn't a game of "if me, then you"
I've learned I can't control anything you do
I've learned that love never fails... but people will
And we might be done but I love you still

THE SECRET OF THE STARS

I wish that I knew the secrets of the stars
And I could tell them of the love that was ours
And when the moonlight danced on my skin
I wish I could show it my heart held within
When I feel the kiss of the ocean
I want it to know of my devotion
So when I feel the drops of rain
I know it will understand my pain

THE PLACE IN YOUR HEART

Take me to the place in your heart where no one has
     been before
Let me find my way around and take a moment
     to explore
I want to carve my initials there and make it
     mine forever more
And you will always know that it is you I adore

EVEN THOUGH YOU CAN'T SEE

To know the anguish of the rain
To feel so deeply all this pain
And still continue on
To make it one more time till dawn
Each and every time you fall
You get up to face it all
Each and every time you call... God's answer
        is the same:
"This pain will end even though you can't see
You my child, You are important to me"

GOODBYE

You said thank you to my goodbye
And all I could do is let out a big sigh
It was what I had come to fear all along
That you were more sick with me... I had hoped
    I was wrong
But the evidence would show that this is true
That I'm part of the problem when it comes to you
So this act of love is a goodbye
And a desperate, angry, sad sigh

COUNT THE COST

How do I count the cost?
Should I count it by time with my loved ones lost?
When I was too tired, and didn't feel good
When I laid down instead of doing what I should
How do I count the cost?
Should I count it by the money lost?
Money spent on addiction, and things to make me
      feel ok
Money not earned, and frittered away
How do I count the cost?
Should I count it by the freedoms lost?
Driving, jail time, house arrest
Promotions not given, jobs lost, 'cause "that" was
      my best
How do I count the cost?
Should I count the life I lost?
Liver damage, ulcers, a life cut short
Or a lifetime in prison ordered by the court
Or should I count it by anger, depression, anxiety,
And excuses
A life out of control, a life of abuses
My life is over I am dead in the ground
There is no one left to hear I am sorry, there is no one
      around
All I loved, all I held dear was lost...
Everything was the cost

HARD LESSONS

How can I miss what used to be
When it didn't exist, it was just a fantasy
Look at the truth... or what I thought it to be
Those are the choices left to me
Both are painful, sad, and make me
      want to scream
Say goodbye to the happiness say goodbye
      to the dream
Say goodbye to the pain, cruelty, and lies
Wipe the streaming, salty tears from my eyes
Learn these hard lessons etch them on my heart
Take responsibility for myself and my part
Pick up the mess, all those pieces lying around
The shattered pieces of my heart on the ground

I WISH I KNEW

I wish I knew the song that the universe sings
And how to measure the length of an angel's wings
Why the cold can burn like a flame
Or why joy and sorrow can ache just the same
Or how our wishes are granted by the falling stars
And how I was blessed with a love like ours

DISAPPOINTMENT

I can feel the fury of my heart as disappointment
     wins the day
And I find myself one more time having to
     walk away
The battle was lost, but not the war
I want retribution, and to settle the score
I want to shake the pillars of the earth and bring him
     to his knees
I want to hear him cry and beg "please"
Disappointment thinks it knows me...
I haven't yet begun to fight
But you can bet my cross hairs are on him,
     I have set him in my sight
So disappointment, this is your warning,
     you should start to run
Cause' I'm hunting you till the last of
     the setting suns

LOVE THE SAME WAY

I want to love the same way the waves try to consume
  the shore
And every time they slip away they keep coming back
  for more
I want to love the same way time tries to
  hold each day
Counting the hours and minutes as they slip away
Until the last second is gone and then...
Time joyously starts to count again
I want to love the same way lyrics love a tune,
Dancing a dance that once it ends, it can't
  start again too soon
I want to love with a fiery passion that roars
  white hot, then ends
Then I want to start all over and do it once again

JUST TO BE

Just to be
It's hard for me
To breathe, exist, and feel,
Seek connection and heal
To love and be enough.
Fitting in is tough
Knowing more than you should know
Keeping quiet, and letting go.
Look, seek, but never find
Quiet voice, loud mind
Hating them all but loving each one
Trying hard to have some fun.

MY HEART AND HEAD

You can close your eyes to what you
        don't want to see
But you can't close your heart to what you
        don't want to feel
It takes a long time for hearts to heal
You can't know what you don't want to learn
And still my heart will long and yearn
The future holds a day I'm longing to see
When my heart and my head both agree

WALKING THE GLOOM

Where she walks no flowers bloom
It's cold and dark and full of gloom
She searches for someone else who sees
Someone she won't make ill at ease
Until she finds them she walks the gloom
The place that no flowers bloom

SONG OF SILENCE

I write my pain on the darkness with black ink
        so no one can see
All the ugly, that is inside of me
I dance in the storm and let the
        rain run down my face
No one can see the difference between them,
        as the tears and rain drops race
I sing a song of silence that only the stars can hear
I sing about my loneliness, sadness and fear
People see the surface and believe that it's all ok
They don't have to look too deep,
        see the pain and look away
Where is the one who understands,
        the one who steps into the gap?
The one who shows up and has your back?
That's the one I am looking for
The one who will help me forget my before

THANK YOU FOR NOTICING

You saw what others looked right through
You noticed the details elusive and few
You heard what no one else could hear
My pain, apprehension, my reticence and fear
You calmed and soothed my tortured soul
It had a thousand wounds and a gaping hole
You kissed each one, you didn't condemn
And when I asked, you did it again...
You helped me mend my broken heart
Brought the pieces together that had come apart

PERCY

Percy the dragon just rescued me from a knight
Yes... yes, you heard me right
Not the way most stories start
But that knight was an arrogant, pompous old fart
I am not like most damsels in distress
I don't have fancy hair or a long dress
So, when Percy the dragon came along and offered to
     take me away...
I jumped up and screamed, "Hip, hip, hooray!"
I climbed up on his back and held on tight
He sprang into the air and we took flight
I loved the way we swooped and rode the air
I left behind every threat, worry and care
We flew to a mountain far, far away
To a castle with a moat, where I plan to stay
We have become the best of friends, the dragon and I
We play games, read books, and go for a fly
I know that it is not what most girls would want
     or choose
But they haven't walked a mile in my shoes
They don't know what it's like to have a dragon as
     your best friend
Loyal and true to the end
You have to be careful of wild sparks and flames,
     it's true
A small price to pay for the lucky few
Who can call a dragon their friend

A MAN WORTH KNOWING

Don't give me a knight in shining armor whose mettle
    has never been tested
Give me the man who gets up every time,
    he's been bested
The man who knows he's broken,
    whose biggest battle is within
Who isn't afraid to look too closely at his sin
The one who knows the truth and integrity well
And for it, a million dollars he wouldn't sell
His word is his bond, you can count on him
He knows where he is going and where
    he has been
A man who appreciates the sweetness of each day
Because of past sorrow and the price he has paid
He is a man worth knowing, the one you
    want to call friend
The one you will stand with till the end

ABOUT THE AUTHOR

Carol Jacobson

Carol is old enough to know better and young enough to still contemplate trying. She enjoys spending time with family and friends and has called the Pacific Northwest home for most of her life. Carol writes most of her poetry on her iPhone... actually, all of it. When she isn't writing, she spends time working as a hairdresser.

Carol plays Texas hold 'em twice a week with the boys at the VFW and enjoys reading a lot. She loves cooking and owns over 100 cookbooks... so she has put herself on cookbook-buying restriction. Since she lives in Seattle, drinking coffee is a hobby... lots and lots of coffee. And she enjoys traveling... but not too far.

www.ingramcontent.com/pod-product-compliance
Lightning Source LLC
Chambersburg PA
CBHW032102080426
42733CB00006B/378